30 Days of Meditation

Fun Techniques for Beginners

Copyright © 2013 by Inbar Shahar

First edition, 2013

As "thank you" for purchasing this book, I want to give you **a gift absolutely 100% FREE!**

Relaxation meditation

http://www.inpeacenow.com/relaxation-meditation.html

To Gurumayi Chidvilasananda with love and gratitude

Contents

Disclaimer: This workbook content is shared from the author's knowledge and experience, and she holds no responsibility for outcomes from following it.

Preface

In 2000, a friend invited me to a meditation center in Los Angeles, CA. I was going through some tough times, and she thought it would help me feel better. I asked her what they do at a meditation center, and when she said chanting and meditating, I thought, "How boring!" She had to convince me over a few weeks to join her, and eventually, I said yes! Little did I know, that night would change my life.

The energy in the room and the repetition of the mantra "Om Namah Shivaya" relaxed me, and finally my mind was clear. I remember saying to her after the program, "There is something in the air. I can feel it. Now I get it. It's all about inner satisfaction." I have tears of gratitude in my eyes remembering that night. I am grateful for my spiritual teacher and the shift in consciousness that meditation has brought into my life. I hope you experience the power of your own inner self and realize how magnificent you are!

Namaste,

Inbar

Introduction

In this book, we will introduce you to the practice of meditation and lead you through a fun 30 day adventure of adding meditation into your daily life. You will learn basic meditation techniques, chakra meditation, mantra meditation, and variety of other types. By the end of the month, you should feel relaxed, focused, and re-energized. After 30 days, meditation should be a habit for you. As you continue to meditate, you and your life will benefit. Soon, you may even crave meditation.

What is meditation?

Meditation is the act of conscious thought. There are many ways to meditate, and in this book, we will be introducing you to a number of easy, helpful techniques.

What are the benefits of meditation?

Meditation reduces stress and increases mental focus. High levels of stress can damage both your mental and physical health. You can expect to find your overall wellbeing improved through daily mediation. You will find that you have more energy for what you want to do as well as improved ability to concentrate on tasks.

When should I meditate?

Meditating before you start your day will give you the energy and focus of a cup of coffee without any negative side effects. However, you may meditate any time of day. It is recommended that you meditate every day, preferably in the same place at the same time. This may not be possible, so focus on finding a time that works best for you each day. Do not stress if you have to change your meditation schedule. Walking meditations and mindfulness can be practiced as you go through your daily activities too.

Where should I meditate?

You may want to create a special area in your home to meditate. You can create an altar with candles, incense, photos of loved ones, images of religious significance, or even an indoor fountain. You may prefer to find a place outside to mediate where you feel close to nature. There are no limits on where you can meditate. Find a place that works for you.

How should I meditate?

Sit in a way that is comfortable for you, and wear clothing that you can relax in. A common meditation posture is an erect back with crossed legs, but this may not be possible or sustainable for you. Find a position that lets you relax and focus. Do not worry how well you are doing, since stressing will lose the point of exercising. Trust the process. Come to it with good intention, and you are certain to be successful.

What types of meditations are there?

All rivers lead to the ocean, and the same goes for meditation. The goal is to change your consciousness, and there are many ways to do so. We will be introducing you to the basics and several different types of meditation.

As with most exercises, you have to practice to increase your endurance, and since meditation exercises your mind, it is important to pace yourself. We will start with two short 3 minute meditations a day, increasing to 10 minutes at once the second week, 15 minutes the third week, and 20 minutes for our final stretch. If you would like to meditate longer, you may, but listen to your body and know your limits. It is recommended to shut off your phone during meditation, though you may wish to set an alarm for the time length, allowing you to relax instead of watching the clock.

In the first week, we will introduce you to breathing and mindfulness techniques. The second week will be chakra mediation, balancing your seven chakras. The third week features mantra meditation, and we will have a variety of meditations during the fourth week. To total 30 days, our last week will be 9 days long ending with a day of mindfulness. Let us begin your journey now!

Week One: Breathing and Mindfulness

Welcome to your first week of meditation! We will begin your journey with an introduction to breathing and mindfulness. These serve as the basis for effective meditation. Learning to breathe consciously is the first step, while mindfulness is learning to think consciously. Each day will include a mindful activity for you to practice. A daily inspirational quote is also given to share what prominent figures have said about meditation and its benefits.

We are starting slowly with 3 minutes of meditation twice a day, but over the next month, you will begin to build your focus and endurance in meditation. Avoid straining yourself. Pay attention to how your body feels. Meditation should be an energizing experience.

Day 1

Breathing

Mindful activity for the day: Notice how often you smile.

Daily quote: *Remember what people used to say about meditation? Now everyone is doing it.* - Shirley MacLaine

Time of meditation: Two 3 minute meditations, repeat the below meditation twice

Find a quiet place to sit comfortably. Set an alarm for 3 minutes if you wish. Notice your breath. Feel the air come in, expanding your lungs and invigorating you. Feel the release and relaxation as you let the air out. Now, place your hands right above your bellybutton. We are going to take several deep breaths. You are going to feel your hands move as you inhale and exhale. Close your eyes if you wish or focus on a calming image.

Breathe in through your nose. Feel your chest expand. Breathe out through your mouth. Breathe in. Breathe out. You feel the tension of your day as you breathe in. Breathe out. Feel that tension slip away. Continue this pattern of breathing deeply. Settle into a rhythm that works for you. You feel the air filling your lungs, and the oxygen awakening your mind. You feel renewed. When you are ready, allow yourself to return your attention to your surroundings. You are ready to continue your day. You may return to this breathing exercise as you need to throughout the day, but we recommend you do at least two 3 minute sessions.

Day 2

Circle breathing

Mindful activity for the day: Count your blessings.

Daily quote: *Every day I try to do breathing exercises, meditation, and yoga. These things sound awfully cliché, but they help me slow down and try to point to a truth.* - David Duchovny

Time of meditation: Two 3 minute meditations, repeat the below meditation twice

Circle breathing is the act of breathing in through your nose and out through your mouth. You already practiced this yesterday, but we are going to focus on this cycle of breathing today. As before, find a comfortable place to sit and set an alarm as needed. You may close your eyes if you wish.

Breathe in through your nose for four counts, "One, two, three, four." Try holding the breath in for four counts, "One, two, three, four." Exhale through your mouth for four counts, "One, two, three, four." You should have felt your body begin to relax. Repeat this cycle. In through the nose, "One, two, three, four." Hold, "One, two, three, four." Release, "one, two, three, four." With each cycle of breathing, you feel your body release built up stress. Your mind starts to clear. Repeat this until the time is up or you are ready to return to your day. You may repeat throughout the day as needed. I always recommend this type of breathing before a stressful event, such as a public presentation, since it helps you release anxiety and regain focus.

Day 3

Alternate breathing

Mindful activity for the day: Draw a picture. Scribble if you want. Have fun!

Daily quote: *One way to look at meditation is as a kind of intrapsychic technology that's been developed over thousands of years by traditions that know a lot about the mind/body connection.* - Jon Kabat-Zinn

Time of meditation: Two 3 minute meditations, repeat the below meditation twice

Today, we are going to balance our energies by alternating breathing through our nostrils. Breathing through one nostril helps stimulate the functioning of the matching brain hemisphere, and when you alternate between the two nostrils, you increase communication between the two halves of your brain, improving overall brain function. This is a great way to quickly find balance on a busy day.

Find a comfortable place to sit. Set an alarm if needed. Place your thumb or index finger on your left nostril, closing it. Breathe in through your right nostril. Now, switch your finger to close your right nostril, and exhale out of your left nostril. Inhale through your left nostril. Move your finger to close your left nostril, and breathe out through your right nostril. Repeat this pattern until you feel complete or the time is up. Do this twice today for three minutes each, but you may repeat more as you wish.

Day 4

Mindfulness

Mindful activity for the day: Let your body guide you into a stretch. If it looks funny, laugh and do it anyway.

Daily quote: *The first recipe for happiness is: avoid too lengthy meditation on the past.* - Andre Maurois

Time of meditation: Two 3 minute meditations, repeat the below meditation twice

Find a quiet place where you will not be disturbed. Set an alarm for 3 minutes if you wish. Sit and let your body relax. Find the rhythm of deep breathing that worked best for you yesterday. Breathe in. Breathe out. Be aware of your breath as we continue the meditation. Close your eyes. Let the muscles in your face relax. Release the tension in your jaw. To release tension in your neck, let your head hang forward, and then roll it gently around, stretching your neck muscles.

We are going to empty your mind. Empty it of worries. Empty it of cares. We are going to let go. With your eyes closed, feel your mind become a void. Let your concerns and stress slip away. You may wish to visualize darkness or light filling your mind. This is not a painful emptiness. It is a soothing absence of thought. Your mind is calm. Become aware of your body. Notice your breath and heartbeat. Breathe and relax in the silence until you are ready to open your eyes. Repeat again for three minutes later in the day.

Day 5

Mindfulness Games

Mindful activity for the day: Try something new. Notice how it makes you feel.

Daily quote: *I practice transcendental meditation and there is a phase where you're meant to lift off the ground. -* Heather Graham

Time of meditation: Two 3 minute meditations, repeat the below meditation twice

Yesterday, you learned the basics of mindfulness by clearing your mind. However, sometimes it can be difficult to clear your mind of thoughts. Today we are going to introduce some practices that free your mind of intrusive thoughts and feelings.

Find a quiet place, make yourself comfortable, and set your alarm. Close your eyes and begin the breathing exercise that works best for you. Let yourself relax as we get ready to clear your mind. Feel your mind start to empty. When a thought pops up disrupting this process, we want to acknowledge it, and then, let it go. You can imagine it vanishing, or if the thought remains, use one of these two visualizations to help release it. The first is you can imagine tying your thought to a balloon and releasing the balloon to fly away. Feel the thought float out of your mind. If that does not work for you, imagine you are wrapping a present. Place your thought into the box and wrap it up. Then set it aside for later. Repeat this process until your mind is emptied of thoughts and concerns. Enjoy the calmness of your mind. When you are ready, open your eyes.

Day 6

Image Meditation

Mindful activity for the day: Look at yourself in the mirror and say, "I love you."

Daily quote: *Through meditation and by giving full attention to one thing at a time, we can learn to direct attention where we choose.* –Eknath Easwaran

Time of meditation: Two 3 minute meditations, repeat the below meditation twice

Today we will practice the mindful contemplation of an image. You may select whatever you would like to look at, something you find calming and positive. Your image could be a painting, a computer desktop, the view out of your window, or a blank wall. Sit yourself comfortably before your selected image and begin your breathing exercise of choice.

Look at the image. Do not strain your eyes. Let your eyes rest on it. See the features of the image. Your eyes slide over it, recognizing the beauty in the image. Notice details you may have missed with a hurried glance. Only focus on the image, so all other thoughts are let go. Be in the now. When you are ready, you may return your attention to your surroundings. You can use this practice of image meditation when you are in situations where closing your eyes for extended times may not be possible or if you see a sight you would like to remember.

Day 7

Day of Practice

Mindful activity for the day: Bless your money.

Daily quote: *Meditation is such a more substantial reality than what we normally take to be reality.* - Richard Gere

Time of meditation: Two 3 minute meditations, repeat the below meditation twice

Today is a day of practice. You are to combine the exercises of the past week in a way that works best for you. Here are some combinations for inspiration:

- Are you an artist looking for ideas? Practice image meditation with alternate nostril breathing to stimulate your mind.

- Big day tomorrow, but you can't sleep? Try emptying your mind using the balloon visualization while circle breathing. Imagine the balloon with your thought floating away as you exhale.

- Has someone upset you? Find your center through mindfulness. Breathe deeply as you clear your mind. Acknowledge your feelings as they arise, but then dismiss them.

You have completed your first week of meditation! You should feel more relaxed throughout your day and know when works best for you to meditate. Next week, you will want to schedule 10 minutes a day as we balance your chakras.

Week Two: *Chakra* Meditation

A *chakra* is a center of the body's energies in Hindu and Buddhist tantrism. In most popular traditions, there are seven major *chakras*. The *chakras* are located along the vertical axis of the body, running from the base of the spine to the top of the head. Each *chakra* is associated with different energies, organs, and color.

Throughout this week, we will introduce you to each *chakra*. You will learn to locate it within your body and realign its energy through meditation. Aligning your *chakras* should bring the benefit of improved physical health and overall wellbeing. Each day will also feature a mindful activity to do, an inspirational quote about meditation, and a brief meditation that you can try on your own.

We will be introducing the *chakras* to you gradually, but once you learn all seven, you can combine them together into a longer meditation. We are meditating 10 minutes at a time this week. Be mindful of your body's reactions. Take breaks as needed and avoid pushing yourself too hard.

Day 8

The Root *Chakra*

Mindful activity for the day: Walk barefoot as much as possible. Sense the ground beneath your feet. Feel grounded.

Daily quote: *Meditation can help us embrace our worries, our fear, our anger; and that is very healing. We let our own natural capacity of healing do the work.* - Thich Nhat Hanh

Time of meditation: 10 minutes

Muladhara, the root *chakra*, is located at the base of your spine. It is often represented by the color red, and it is associated with the lower digestive tract and the element Earth. When your root *chakra* is in balance, you feel grounded and secure. However, when disrupted, it can lead to gastrointestinal disturbance and mental health issues from feeling ungrounded. Let us ground your root *chakra* with the following meditation:

Sit in a comfortable position with your back erect. Take a deep breath, stretching your spine as you breathe in. Let go. Relax. Close your eyes. Continue to breathe deeply and slowly. Clear your mind until there is only a calm void. Now, imagine your body. See yourself sitting, back erect. Focus on the base of your spine. You see a soft red glow at the base. Look closer. You see the red glow grow, so that its warming light encompasses your lower abdomen. The light embraces your lower back muscles and large intestine. The light forms roots that reach down from your spine, connecting you with the Earth below. You are grounded. You are part of the Earth. Continue this visualization and breathing until you are ready to open your eyes.

Day 9

The Sacral *Chakra*

Mindful activity for the day: Compliment your partner, a family member, or a friend today.

Daily quote: *The flowering of love is meditation.* - Jiddu Krishnamurti

Time of meditation: 10 minutes

Swadhisthana, the sacral *chakra*, is located between your tailbone and pubic bone, right above the root *chakra*. It is often represented by the color orange, and it is associated with the sexual organs and the element Water. When your sacral *chakra* is in balance, you feel outgoing and content. However, when disrupted, it can lead to hormonal imbalance, sexual dysfunction, and urinary tract problems. Let us refocus your sacral *chakra* with the following meditation:

Sit in a comfortable position with your back erect. Take a deep breath, release the tension in your shoulders. Relax. Close your eyes. Continue to breathe deeply and slowly. Clear your mind until there is only a calm void. Now, imagine your body. See yourself sitting, back erect. Focus on the base of your spine. You see a soft red glow at the base. Now, look above the root *chakra* to find the orange glow of the sacral *chakra*. You see the orange glow pulse, its light reaching out from your lower back muscles to embrace your bladder and sexual organs. The orange light courses through your organs like water, washing away all blockages in your system. You are cleansed and revitalized. You are Water. Continue this visualization and breathing until you are ready to open your eyes.

Day 10

The Solar Plexus *Chakra*

Mindful activity for the day: Pamper yourself. Do something you enjoy.

Daily quote: *"Recognize that you have the courage within you to fulfill the purpose of your birth. Summon forth the power of your inner courage and live the life of your dreams."* - Gurumayi Chidvilasananda

Time of meditation: 10 minutes

Manipura, the solar plexus *chakra*, is located at your navel. It is often represented by the color yellow, and it is associated with the digestive organs and the element Fire. When your solar plexus *chakra* is in balance, you feel focused and confident. However, when disrupted, it can lead to digestive disturbance, unregulated blood sugar, and poor self-image. Let us refocus your solar plexus *chakra* with the following meditation:

Sit in a comfortable position with your back erect. Take a deep breath, release the tension in your shoulders. Relax. Close your eyes. Continue to breathe deeply and slowly. Clear your mind until there is only a calm void. Now, imagine your body. See yourself sitting, back erect. Focus on your spine. You see the red and orange glows, and above is a bright yellow light. The yellow glow extends from your bellybutton back to your spine. Its light is strong. You may wish to place your hands over your belly button to feel its warmth. You feel your body's energy focusing here. Your digestive tract is soothed and healthy. You feel self-assured. You are energized and confident. You are fueled by Fire. Continue this visualization and breathing until you are ready to open your eyes.

Day 11

The Heart *Chakra*

Mindful activity for the day: Bless everyone in the whole universe. Feel your heart expand.

Daily quote: *If we have no peace, it is because we have forgotten that we belong to each other.* - Mother Teresa

Time of meditation: 10 minutes

Anahata, the heart *chakra*, is located at the level of your heart. It is often represented by the color green, and it is associated with the circulatory system and the element Air. When your heart *chakra* is in balance, you feel loving and connected. However, when disrupted, it can lead to breathing problems, poor circulation, and feeling unloved. Let us refocus your heart *chakra* with the following meditation:

Sit in a comfortable position with your back erect. Take a deep breath, release the tension in your shoulders. Relax. Close your eyes. Continue to breathe deeply and slowly. Clear your mind until there is only a calm void. Now, imagine your body. See yourself sitting, back erect. You see the red, orange, and yellow of your lower back. Your eyes follow up to your heart. Your heart is filled with a gentle green glow of a growing plant. The green glow pulses from your heart, through your body's arteries, reaching even the smallest capillaries. Your lungs expand with your breath, and you see the green light fill them. You are Air. You encompass the world. You are love. Continue this visualization and breathing until you are ready to open your eyes.

Day 12

The Throat *Chakra*

Mindful activity for the day: Sing a song that brings you joy.

Daily quote: *The purpose of our lives is to be happy.* - Dalai Lama

Time of meditation: 10 minutes

Vishuddha, the throat *chakra*, is located at the back of your neck. It is often represented by the color blue, and it is associated with Sound, encompassing the throat, ears and mouth. When your throat *chakra* is in balance, you feel positive and creative. However, when disrupted, it can lead to neck pain and hearing problems. Let us refocus your throat *chakra* with the following meditation:

Sit in a comfortable position with your back erect. Take a deep breath, release the tension in your shoulders. Relax. Close your eyes. Continue to breathe deeply and slowly. Clear your mind until there is only a calm void. Now, imagine your body. See yourself sitting, back erect. Focus on your spine. Your eyes travel up it. You see red, orange, yellow, green, and then as your reach your neck, blue. A bright cheerful blue is coming from your neck and shining out from your throat. You have voice. You can hear. Sound fills you with positive energy. Say, "Om." As you speak, close your mouth at the end, allowing the sound to reverberate through your throat and up into your head. The blue light pulses with the sound, filling your throat, mouth and ears. Your mind is filled with creative energy and you are focused. Continue this visualization and repeat "Om" until you are ready to open your eyes.

Day 13

The Third Eye *Chakra*

Mindful activity for the day: Watch your thoughts throughout the day. How much was positive?

Daily quote: *Meditation is all about the pursuit of nothingness. It's like the ultimate rest. It's better than the best sleep you've ever had. It's a quieting of the mind. It sharpens everything, especially your appreciation of your surroundings. It keeps life fresh.* - Hugh Jackman

Time of meditation: 10 minutes

Ajna, the third eye *chakra*, is located between your eyebrows, where your nose meets your forehead. It is often represented by the color indigo, and it is associated with your eyes, brain, and the element Light. When your third eye *chakra* is in balance, you feel in control and intuitive. However, when disrupted, it can lead to headaches and distorted reality. Let us refocus your third eye *chakra* with the following meditation:

Sit in a comfortable position with your back erect. Take a deep breath, release the tension in your shoulders. Relax. Close your eyes. Continue to breathe deeply and slowly. Clear your mind until there is only a calm void. Now, imagine your body. See yourself sitting, back erect. Focus on your spine. You see red, orange, yellow, green, blue, and between your eyes, an indigo glow. The bluish purple light shines brightly from your third eye. Here is your intuition. You are guided through life by the light. The indigo light soothes your mind. Your mind is calm, free of anxiety or doubt. You know your path. Continue this visualization until you are ready to open your eyes.

Day 14

The Crown *Chakra*

Mindful activity for the day: Do something kind for a stranger.

Daily quote: *You must not lose faith in humanity. Humanity is an ocean; if a few drops of the ocean are dirty, the ocean does not become dirty.* - Mahatma Gandhi

Time of meditation: 10 minutes

Sahasrara, the crown *chakra*, is located at the top of your head. It is often represented by the color violet. The crown *chakra* holds the power of Thought. When your crown *chakra* is in balance, your mind is open and you are one with the universe. However, when disrupted, you may feel lost, dull and tired. Let us refocus your crown *chakra* with the following meditation:

Sit in a comfortable position with your back erect. Take a deep breath, release the tension in your shoulders. Relax. Close your eyes. Continue to breathe deeply and slowly. Clear your mind until there is only a calm void. Now, imagine your body. See yourself sitting, back erect. Focus on your spine. You see the colors of the rainbow glowing as they flow up your spine ending with a violet glow from the top of your head. The violet glows brighter until it shines white. The white light is entering your body from the top of your head. You feel the white light pour down through your body. Calming you. Cooling you. Connecting you. You are whole. You are One. Continue this visualization until you are ready to open your eyes.

Your *chakras* are now balanced.

Week Three: Mantra Meditation

The word "mantra" refers to a sound, word, or phrase repeated during meditation. A mantra allows you to focus your energies and expand your consciousness. The repetition of a mantra is helpful in achieving a mindful state. Mantras can serve as prayers or invocations, allowing you to send a message and positive energy into the shared consciousness.

For this third week, we will begin with mantras of words you may be familiar with. We will then introduce several Sanskrit mantras that are commonly used in Buddhist and Hindu meditation. Finally, we will let you select mantras that are personally meaningful to you from prayers, poems, and songs.

Each meditation this week will last fifteen minutes. Since these meditations may include vocalizing, it is important to find a space where you feel comfortable making sounds if you wish to do so. The reverberations of the sounds through your body are a part of mantra meditation's benefits. However, you may find that you enjoy and get more benefit from repeating the mantra within your mind. So for this week's meditations that refer to speaking aloud, you may wish to try speaking them aloud first, then switch to saying them internally. You may want to place a glass of water near you in case you need it. Remember to not force yourself, and you may pause at any point. Now, let us begin mantra meditation!

Day 15

"Peace"

Mindful activity for the day: Think of someone that challenges you and send them a blessing – notice how you feel inside. Do not judge yourself, just notice. Any action where we bless others and open our hearts will expand our awareness.

Daily quote: *If you hate a person, you hate something in him that is part of yourself. What isn't part of ourselves doesn't disturb us.* - Hermann Hesse

Time of meditation: 15 minutes

Today is a day of peace. In your mindful activity for today, we asked that you think of someone that challenges you. If you would like to add to your healing process, you may hold that person in mind as we practice our "peace" mantra today.

Find a comfortable place to sit, legs folded or feet placed firmly on the floor. Set an alarm if necessary. Close your eyes and take a deep breath. Find a steady rhythm for your breathing. Now, within your mind, speak the word "Peace." Repeat it several times silently in your mind, allowing it to build in intensity, until you are ready to speak aloud. Feel the sound leave your mouth. Continue to repeat "peace" louder and louder until you find a volume that resonates within you. Take your time with the word, let it flow from your lips. Repeat this mantra until the time is up or you feel fatigued. If you need to pause, stop and take a drink of water. As you leave your meditation, you may wish to say "Amen" or "*Namaste*" in closing.

Day 16

"Peace, Love, Harmony"

Mindful activity for the day: Repeat "peace, love, and harmony" throughout your day. How does it go? Did people treat you differently?

Daily quote: *I have found the paradox, that if you love until it hurts, there can be no more hurt, only more love.* - Mother Teresa

Time of meditation: 15 minutes

Today we will build on the foundation laid yesterday. We will add to our earlier mantra, expanding it to "Peace, Love, Harmony." Find your place to meditate and prepare yourself for fifteen minutes. As with before, if you would like to focus your mantra's energies on blessing another, you may.

Close your eyes. Breathe deeply. Let go. Hear within your mind, "Peace, Love, Harmony." What do those words mean to you? Find calm and strength in them. Repeat them silently until you feel ready to say them aloud. Continue to your preferred volume and let yourself fall into a rhythm. Peace. Love. Harmony. Again. Peace. Love. Harmony. Feel the words. Feel their meaning. Feel at peace. Feel the love in you. Feel at harmony with the world. As before, continue with the mantra until you need to pause or you are ready to stop. You may end with "Amen" or "*Namaste.*"

Day 17

"Om Namah Shivaya"

Mindful activity for the day: Smell a flower or hug a tree. How do you feel? What do you sense?

Daily quote: *"You are a cosmic flower. Om chanting is the process of opening the psychic petals of that flower."* — Amit Ray

Time of meditation: 15 minutes

"Om Namah Shivaya" is one of the most popular mantras for meditation, coming from Hindu meditation. You may recognize the first syllable, "Om," from our throat chakra meditation last week. "Om" is a sacred sound often used to open and close mantras, but you may also use it on its own. Our mantra *"Om Namah Shivaya"* translates to "adoration of Shiva." The Hindu god Shiva represents all at the highest level, so you may understand this mantra as "Love all." Understanding and correct pronunciation are not necessary to reap the benefits of a mantra, so do not fear if this mantra appears complicated at first.

Prepare yourself by sitting comfortably, beginning your breathing exercises, and closing your eyes. Begin with, "Om." Say it aloud. Feel it vibrate through your body. Repeat until you are ready to start the whole mantra. Open your eyes to read it if you need to. Break it down and say it slowly at first, *"Om Na-mah Shi-va-ya."* Find the melody in the mantra. Let the words move through you. *"Om Namah Shivaya."* Continue until you are ready to pause or stop, and allow yourself a moment of silence at the end, feeling the mantra's positive energy soak in.

Day 18

"Om mani padme hum"

OM MANI PADME HUM

Mindful activity for the day: Look at yourself in the mirror with fresh eyes today. Turn your head to different angles. See what you admire. Send yourself love.

Daily quote: *Yoga is a great thing and meditation is also great to get connected to yourself more. -* Ziggy Marley

Time of meditation: 15 minutes

"*Om mani padme hum*" translates from Sanskrit to "Jewel Lotus," and it is an incredibly sacred Buddhist incantation. The lotus is sacred to many Eastern traditions, and it represents purity to Buddhists. Now, to begin your meditation, find your quiet place and make yourself comfortable.

Close your eyes. Breathe in. Let go. Breathe in. Feel the "Om" growing within your chest, and release it with your exhalation. Now, for the mantra, "*Om ma-ni pad-me hum.*" Slowly at first, let yourself feel the movement of the words. See how they move around as if on a wheel, falling into the next repetition. "*Om mani padme hum.*" Feel the energy of the words travel up through your *chakras* exiting from the top of your head. You are connected. You are purified. "*Om mani padme hum.*" Continue to chant this mantra until you feel complete or the fifteen minute ends. Allow yourself a moment of silence before opening your eyes.

Day 19

"Om Loka Samasta Sukino Bhavantu"

Mindful activity for the day: Give a compliment to a coworker or friend.

Daily quote: *It is not our purpose to become each other; it is to recognize each other, to learn to see the other and honor him for what he is.* - Hermann Hesse

Time of meditation: 15 minutes

"Om Loka Samasta Sukino Bhavantu" roughly translates from Sanskrit to "May all the worlds' beings be happy and free of suffering and may I be part of that divine consciousness." During this meditation, try to expand your mind's scope to embrace the worlds you know and can imagine. See yourself as connected through ties of cosmic love and thought.

Find a place to quietly meditate and make yourself comfortable. Once you are ready, close your eyes and begin your preferred breathing exercise. Start with chanting, "Om," and then slowly move into the mantra, *"Om Lo-ka Sa-ma-sta Su-ki-no Bha-van-tu."* You may wish to open your eyes to read the words from this text given its length and complexity. Do not concern yourself with correct pronunciation. Feel the sound of the words resonate through you and that energy connecting you with the life force of those around you. Let the connections grow. Your energy is expanding further with each repetition of the mantra. You are sending positive energy to the cosmos, a cosmos which includes you. When time is up or you are ready to stop, let yourself return you attention to the room slowly, maintaining your sense of connectedness and unity.

Day 20

Prayer/Poem Mantra

Mindful activity for the day: Ask for forgiveness for anyone that you ever hurt, intentionally or not. Ask the forgiveness of yourself for your actions and release any pent up negative energy.

Daily quote: *I deepen my experience of God through prayer, meditation, and forgiveness.* - Marianne Williamson

Time of meditation: 15 minutes

Many of the mantras you have practiced this week originate from Hindu and Buddhist prayers and scriptures. Today we would like you to find a line from a prayer or poem that carries special significance for you. Here are some suggestions if you are having difficulty thinking of one:

- "God, grant me the serenity to accept the things I cannot change, the courage to change the things I can, and wisdom to know the difference." - *Serenity Prayer*, Reinhold Niebuhr

- "Surely goodness and mercy shall follow me all the days of my life: and I will dwell in the house of the Lord forever." – Psalm 23:6, KJV

- "Empty your heart of empty fears. When you get yourself out of the way, I am there." – *I Am There*, James Dillet Freeman

When you are ready, look to the mantra meditations above and begin your meditation, replacing your chose line with an earlier mantra.

Day 21

Song Lyric Mantra

Mindful activity for the day: Do something fun. Ask your soul to guide you.

Daily quote: *At the end of the day, I can end up just totally wacky, because I've made mountains out of molehills. With meditation, I can keep them as molehills.* - Ringo Starr

Time of meditation: 15 minutes

You can find mantras everywhere! The words or sounds used in a mantra merely need to carry positive energy for you. Similar to yesterday, we will have you select a song lyric you enjoy and inspires peace in your heart. Choose one that is important for you. Here are some suggestions to give you an idea of examples:

- "You may say I'm a dreamer, but I'm not the only one, I hope someday you'll join us, and the world will be as one." *Imagine*, John Lennon

- "I wish you joy, And I wish you happiness, But above all this, I wish you love." *I Will Always Love You*, Dolly Parton

- "What the world needs now, Is love, sweet love, No, not just for some but for everyone." *What the World Needs Now is Love*, Burt Bacharach

When you have selected your lyric mantra, practice your mantra meditation as you have learned this week, inserting your chosen mantra. Sing the mantra or speak it. Do what feels most natural to you. I hope you will end this week feeling confident in the use of mantras, knowing you can use words to bring focus to your daily life.

Week Four: Variety

You are now beginning the last week of your guided adventure into meditation. We hope that you are beginning to feel confident in your meditations, and you have established a routine that works well for you. We are increasing the meditation length to 20 minutes a day, though if you need to reduce it or split the time into two, you may. This week will feature a variety of different types of meditations.

Day 22

Zen meditation

Mindful activity for the day: Be kind to an animal today. Smile at your neighbor's cat in the window, pet a dog, or scatter crumbs for the birds.

Daily quote: *The greatness of a nation can be judged by the way its animals are treated.* - Mahatma Gandhi

Time of meditation: 20 minutes

Zen meditation, also known as "*zazen*," is defined by its upright sitting position. For this meditation, you should find a place to sit on the floor. If you would like to use a pillow or sit in a chair, that is acceptable as well. Sit up straight with your legs crossed in a way that is natural for you. Do not strain yourself, but attempt to maintain a straight back posture.

Breathe deep and release. Let your eyes rest on the scene before you. *Zazen* is about mindful observation. Feel your chest rise and fall as you breathe. Close your eyes and quiet your mind. Relax your control. Let your thoughts, concerns and feelings flow through you. Let them come forth, but do not grab onto any of them. Observe them and let go. As they are let go, the thoughts are washed away in the stream of your consciousness. Your mind is now free. Begin to lower your barriers, letting in only positive energy. Feel yourself as part of the universe. Continue to observe quietly until the 20-minute mark has passed. Slowly open your eyes when you are ready.

Day 23

Love Meditation

Mindful activity for the day: Send loving blessings to everyone you meet today.

Daily quote: *Love begins at home, and it is not how much we do... but how much love we put in that action.* - Mother Teresa

Time of meditation: 20 minutes

For this meditation, we are going to practice loving ourselves and sending our love to others. Learning to love and value yourself is a vital part of forming loving relationships with others. For those of us who have been in situations that made us doubt our worthiness of love, we must learn to recognize the divine power within and our innate right to respectful love from others.

Prepare yourself for meditation by finding a quiet, comfortable place to sit. For this meditation, you may wish to hold a pillow in your arms. Breathe deep. Exhale. Close your eyes. Clear your mind. Now, contemplate the word, "Love." What is love to you? Who do you love? When do you feel loved? Does love make you feel connected? Find your love. See yourself in your mind. Do you love yourself? Hug the pillow in your arms. The pillow is the child in you that needs love. Send love to yourself. Feel yourself filled with love until you are love. Love radiates from you. Your love expands out to enfold those close to you. If you can, allow your love to expand further to encompass the world. See the bright light of your love illuminating the hearts of all. Hold this image until you are ready to open your eyes.

Day 24

Stone Meditation

Mindful activity for the day: Take a moment to walk around outside. Look at the ground to find a smooth stone that speaks to you for your meditation today.

Daily quote: *Happiness is not something ready made. It comes from your own actions.* - Dalai Lama

Time of meditation: 20 minutes

In your mindful activity for today, you were asked to find a smooth stone outdoors that resonated with you. If you already have a favorite stone, you may use it instead. For this meditation, you will be holding the stone in your hands. It is not required, but you may want to write a meaningful word or the name of someone you wish to pray for on the stone.

Bring your stone with you as you find a quiet place to meditate. As you get comfortable in your seat, cup the stone in your hands, and let your hands rest in your lap. Clear your mind and begin your breathing exercises. You may now turn your attention to your stone. Slowly move your hands over it, feeling the texture of its surface. Observe its color and shape. Know this stone is of the universe. It is composed of atoms, as are you. You are one. Feel the stone begin to warm in your hands. You are sharing your body's energy, infusing the stone with the love inside you. Quietly contemplate the stone until twenty minutes have passed. You may keep the stone to use again, or if you wish, you may give it to someone special to show you care.

Day 25

Nature/Walking Meditation

Mindful activity for the day: Sit outside quietly for five minutes today. Feel the sun on your face if it is out, otherwise watch the movement of the clouds above.

Daily quote: *When you look at the sun during your walking meditation, the mindfulness of the body helps you to see that the sun is in you; without the sun there is no life at all and suddenly you get in touch with the sun in a different way.* - Thich Nhat Hanh

Time of meditation: 20 minutes

Today's meditation asks you to walk outside, so ideally, locate a walking trail in a green area near your home or place of work. If you do not have access to an area like this or the weather today is not hospitable, find an available environment you find soothing that allows you to walk freely, such as the local library or a shopping mall. Make sure you are wearing comfortable walking shoes.

On arriving, pause and take a deep breath. Feel the air fill your lungs, invigorating you. Begin to walk very slowly. You do not have to have a destination. Allow your body to lead you where it wishes to go. Avoid staring at your feet, and focus your attention on your surroundings. Take in what you see. If you see something interesting, pause to quietly observe it. You are in nature. Touch the leaves of the plants and the trunks of trees as you pass them. Continue your walk until twenty minutes have passed. Try to bring this mindfulness to all of your daily walking.

Day 26

Passage Meditation

Mindful activity for the day: Find good news. Look for an uplifting story of human compassion in your paper, TV or online news source.

Daily quote: *The affairs of the world will go on forever. Do not delay the practice of meditation.* - Milarepa

Time of meditation: 20 minutes

You have already practiced some versions of passage meditation with the mantras in Week 3. However, today, we would like you to select a longer passage to read and contemplate. Choose something that you know will be uplifting.

Once you find your passage, find a quiet place to sit and read. As you read through the text, pause and allow the meaning of the words to sink in. This is not a race. You are not in a rush. You are taking each word in one at a time. If you reach the end of your passage, stop and think quietly for a moment before beginning again. Emotions may arise as you read. Acknowledge the emotions and their origins, then gently let go. Allow yourself a moment at the end of the meditation to close your eyes and let the words settle in your mind. The passage may be from a scripture, a story, or a poem. If you are unable to look up a passage, you may use the poem on the next page.

A Moment of Happiness

A moment of happiness,

you and I sitting on the verandah,

apparently two, but one in soul, you and I.

We feel the flowing water of life here,

you and I, with the garden's beauty

and the birds singing.

The stars will be watching us,

and we will show them

what it is to be a thin crescent moon.

You and I unselfed, will be together,

indifferent to idle speculation, you and I.

The parrots of heaven will be cracking sugar

as we laugh together, you and I.

In one form upon this earth,

and in another form in a timeless sweet land.

\-   Mewlana Jalaluddin Rumi

Day 27

Taoist Meditation

Mindful activity for the day: Tidy up your living and work spaces. Notice how the atmosphere lifts and energy is freed.

Daily quote: *No thought enters the mind, no problems arise from the body, no memories grip the spirit. This overwhelming sense of tranquility is really all meditation is about. The neutral stillness of the mind renews the tired soul, and this is regeneration.* - Deng Ming Dao

Time of meditation: 20 minutes

Taoist meditation shares the mindfulness and breathing exercises of other traditions like zen. However, sitting still is not required. Let your body guide you towards what is needed to achieve relaxation. It may be running, dancing, or even lying down. T'ai Chi Ch'uan and Qi Gong are two examples of Taoist meditation in action, so participate in one of these if you have the chance.

As you move through you actions, maintain the mindful awareness you have learned and breathe. Observe how your body moves. Feel your muscles stretch and contract. Do not rush your movements. Let them flow out through you. Pent-up negative energy is released from your body, healing and re-energizing you. Increase or decrease the intensity and speed of your actions as your body wishes. Though the designated time for this meditation ends after 20 minutes, you are welcome to continue your mindful movement as long as you like.

Day 28

Sense meditation

Mindful activity for the day: Eat mindfully. Taste each bite, and chew slowly, savoring it before swallowing. You may find that you do not overeat as easily doing this.

Daily quote: *As a body everyone is single, as a soul never.* - Hermann Hesse

Time of meditation: 20 minutes

Sense meditation focuses on calming your five physical senses, allowing your body to open up to other experiences. You will learn to tune into your body. Sense meditation is helpful when you are unable to find a quiet place to be alone, but need to re-center yourself.

Find a comfortable place to sit. Breathe deeply and relax. We are going to begin with sight. Look straight ahead, and slowly lower your eyelids until your eyes are closed. Moving down your face, we find your sense of smell. Breathe. As you breathe, do not focus on the smells around you. Let them roll off your awareness. To your mouth and taste, swallow and breathe. You taste nothing. This is not unpleasant, just an absence. For your hearing, imagine warm hands cupping your ears, blocking out external sounds. All you can hear is the quiet of your mind. Lastly, we move to your sense of touch, your skin. Feel your seat beneath you, your clothes on your skin, and slowly pull your attention away from this. Fold into yourself. You are contained. Now you can sense the shining light within. Rest in your quiet, and when you are ready, let the light expand to reignite your senses, leaving you calm and aware.

Day 29

Open eye meditation

Mindful activity for the day: Change your computer desktop to a new image that fills you with peace and joy. Spend a moment contemplating it.

Daily quote: *This is my simple religion. There is no need for temples; no need for complicated philosophy. Our own brain, our own heart is our temple; the philosophy is kindness.* - Dalai Lama

Time of meditation: 20 minutes

Open eye meditation is practiced by selecting two objects, placing them before you, and then having each eye focus on a different object. This type of concentration takes up your mind's focus, making it easier to achieve a meditative state. For the objects, please select items that you find pleasant. You could also consider looking at a wall hanging or quilt that has separate images to focus on.

Position yourself in front of your two items. Close your eyes briefly and breathe. Open your eyes. Let them rest on the two items. Focus your attention on having each eye consider its own item. Let your mind empty out as you do this. There are only these items and you. There are no concerns. There are no worries. Your mind is free, and you can feel the tension lifting from your scalp. Breathe calmly and deeply. When you are ready to come out of the meditation, close your eyes to break the focus, and return to your day calmed.

Day 30

Day of *Vipassana*

Mindful activity for the day: All of your activities today will be mindful!

Daily quote: *We tend to think of meditation in only one way. But life itself is a meditation.* -

Raul Julia

Time of meditation: 20 minutes + day of mindfulness

Today will be a day of *Vipassana*, which is the Buddhist practice of seeing the world as it is. As your final day, we also encourage you to make time for a twenty minute meditation, selecting from your favorite in this book. It would be best to do this meditation first thing in the morning to place you in a mindful state for the day.

For *Vipassana*, you will go through your day in a mindful state. Look at your surroundings. See the details, observe, and let go of pressing thoughts. Be aware of your body and its movements. Feel the ground beneath your feet, but let your body become light and relaxed. If you are at work, do your best work. Your work has meaning. Your work matters. However, know that you and the world continue without it. You are your own. You are free. You are of everything. Smile often today, and send your love to yourself and others!

Conclusion

Thank you so much for sharing this journey with us! We hope that meditation has become part of your daily activities and that your life is benefitting from it. You should be very proud of yourself for taking the initiative to bring focus and light into your life. As my friend introduced me to meditation, I hope that you too may be able to share this gift with others.

The meditations presented throughout this book are only a sample of possibilities. We encourage you to explore meditation further. Be creative! Have fun!

Additional Books by Inbar Shahar

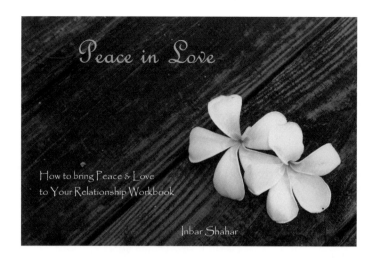

Peace in Love

How to bring Peace & Love
to Your Relationship Workbook

Inbar Shahar

3 steps to Relaxation

A Stress Reduction Workbook

Inbar Shahar

Children's Books

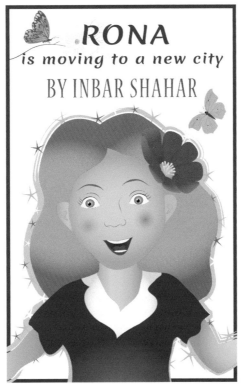

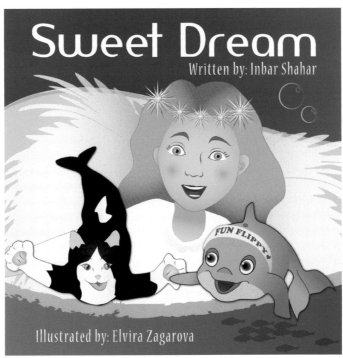

The Magic Tree

Written by: Inbar Shahar

Illustrated by: Elvira Zagarova

FREE VIDEO book inside